Symphony No. 4
in A Major, Op. 90
"Italian"

Felix Mendelssohn

DOVER PUBLICATIONS, INC.
Mineola, New York

Published in Canada by General Publishing Company, Ltd., 30 Lesmill Road, Don Mills, Toronto, Ontario.

Published in the United Kingdom by Constable and Company, Ltd., 3 The Lanchesters, 162–164 Fulham Palace Road, London W6 9ER.

Bibliographical Note

This Dover edition, first published in 1997, is an unabridged republication of *Vierte (italienische) Symphonie, Op. 90*, from "Serie 1. Symphonien für Orchester" in *Felix Mendelssohn Bartholdy's Werke. Kritisch durchgesehene Ausgabe von Julius Rietz. Mit Genehmigung der Originalverleger,* originally published by Breitkopf & Härtel, Leipzig, 1874–77.

International Standard Book Number: 0-486-29953-8

Manufactured in the United States of America
Dover Publications, Inc., 31 East 2nd Street, Mineola, N.Y. 11501

CONTENTS

Symphony No. 4
in A Major, Op. 90
"Italian" (1833)

INSTRUMENTATION

2 Flutes [Flauti]
2 Oboes [Oboi]
2 Clarinets in A [Clarinetti]
2 Bassoons [Fagotti]

2 Horns in E, A [Corni]
2 Trumpets in D, E [Trombe]

Timpani [Timpani, Timp.]

Violins I, II [Violino]
Violas [Viola]
Cellos [Violoncello]
Basses [Basso]

Symphony No. 4
in A Major, Op. 90
"Italian"

Allegro vivace.
Flauti.
Oboi.
Clarinetti in A.
Fagotti.
Corni in A.
Trombe in D.
Timpani in E.A.
Violino I.
Violino II.
Viola.
Violoncello.
Basso.
pizz.
arco
fp
f
sf
p

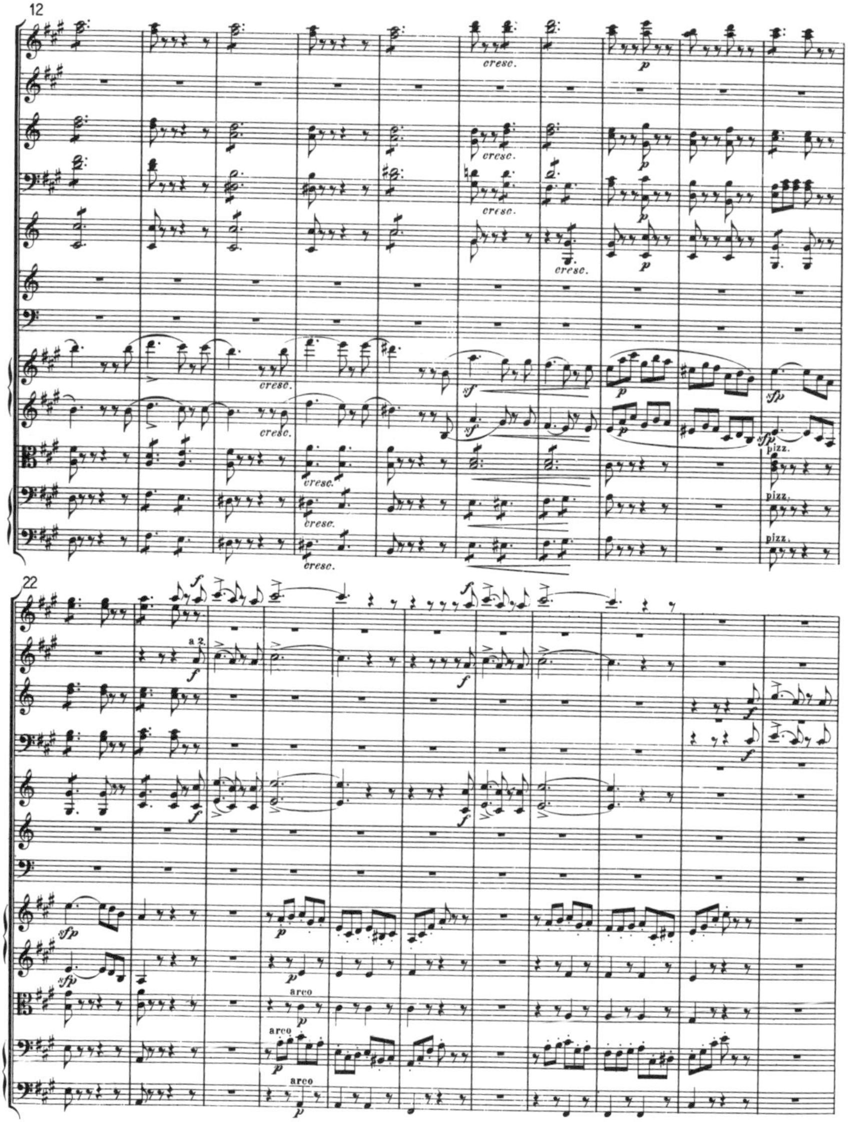
12
cresc.
p
sf
sfp
pizz.
22
a 2.
f
arco

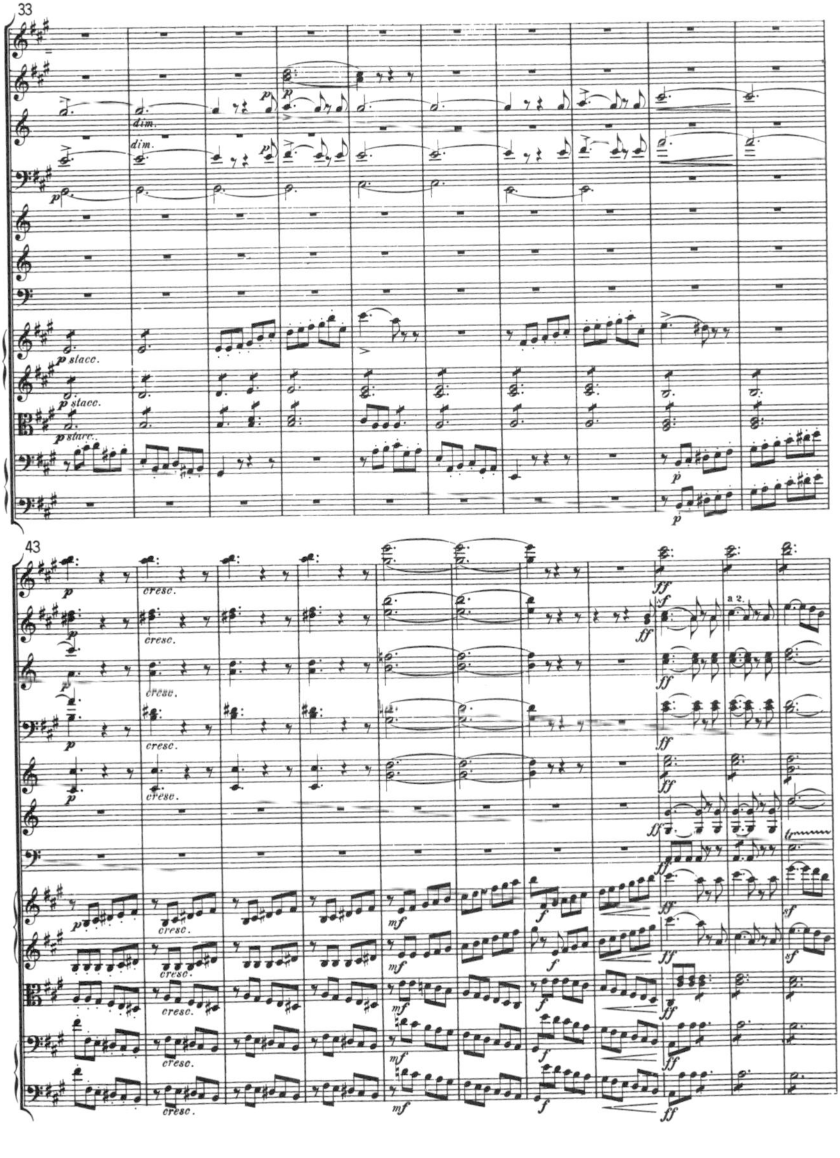
33
dim.
dim.
p
p stacc.
p stacc.
p stacc.
43
cresc.
mf
f
ff
sf
a 2.

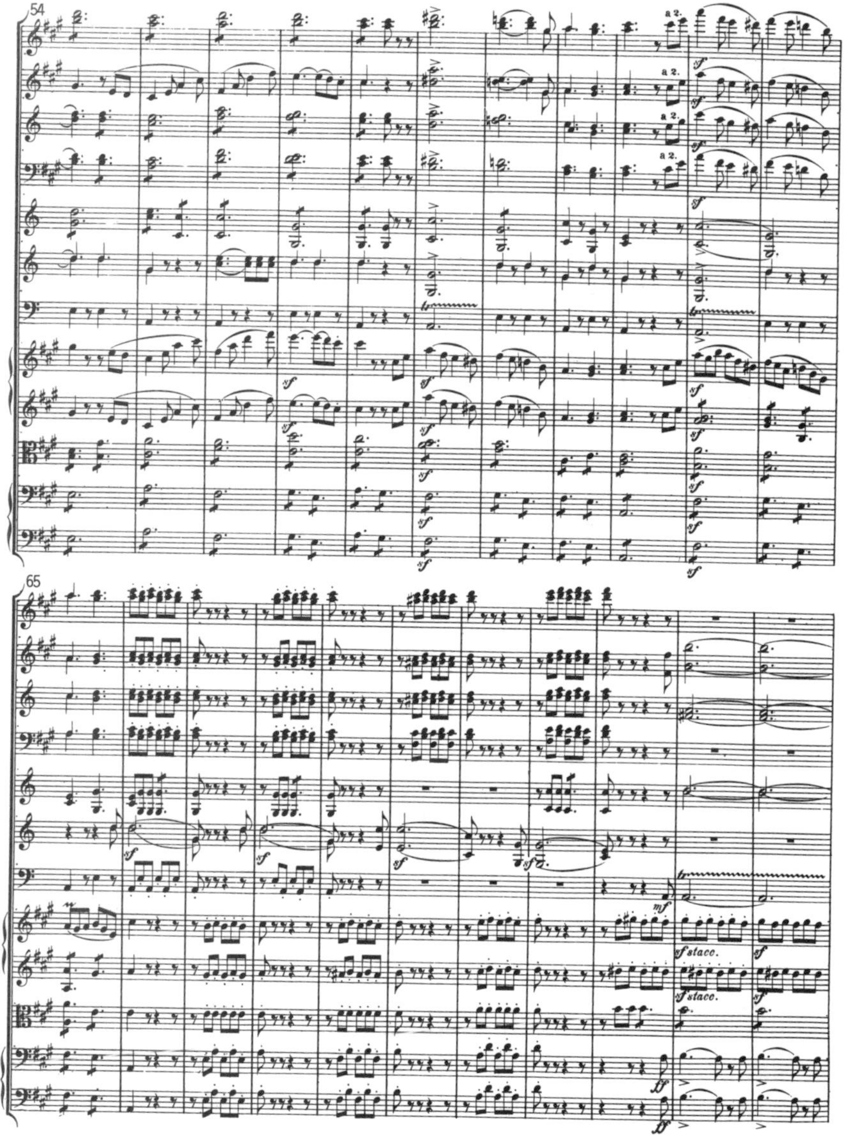
54
a 2.
a 2.
a 2.
a 2.
65
sf staco.
sf staco.
mf
ff

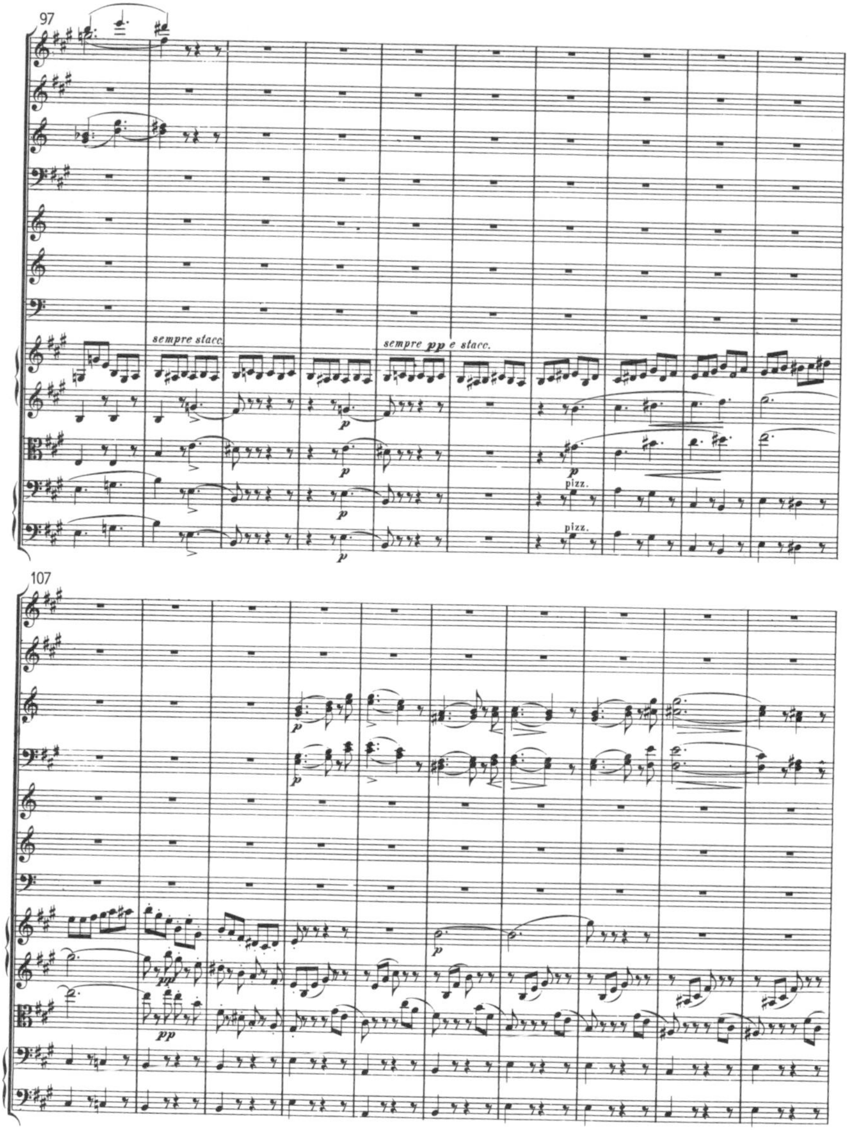
97
sempre stacc.
sempre pp e stacc.
p
pizz.
107
pp

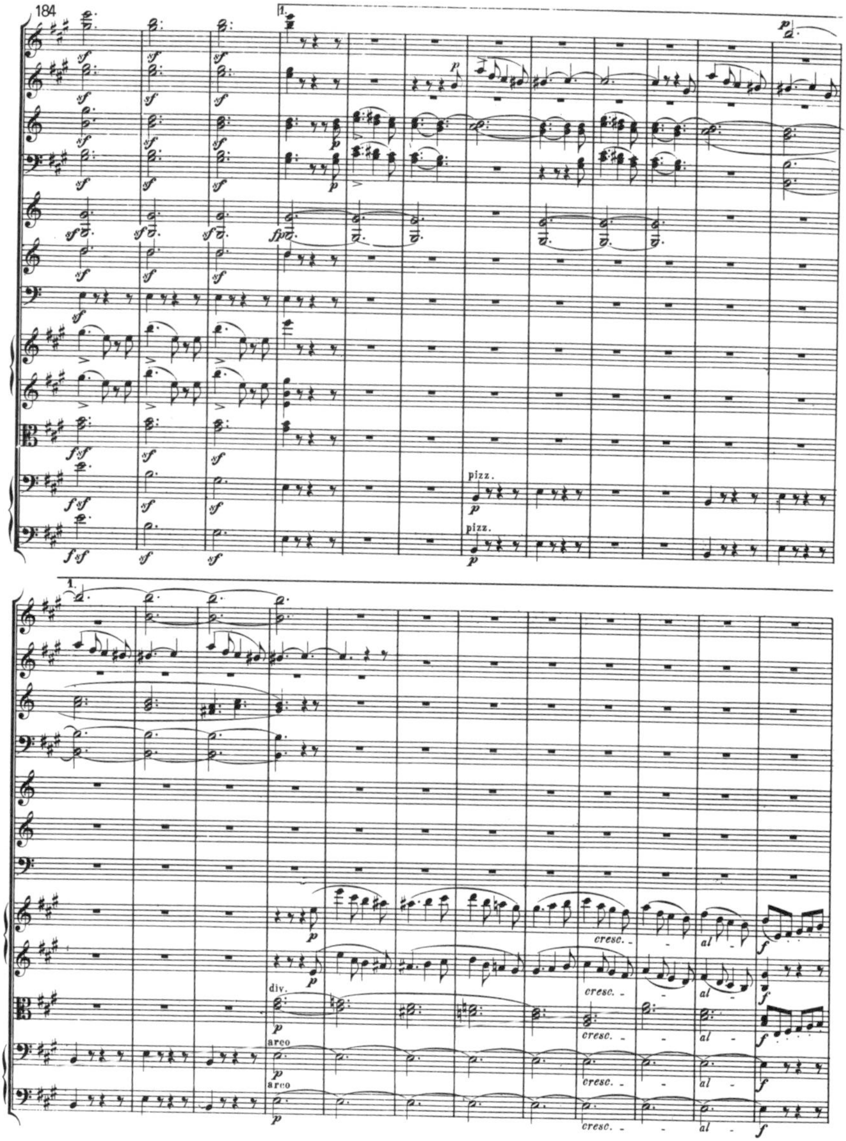
184
1.
sf
fp
p
pizz.
pizz.
1.
div.
arco
arco
cresc.
al
f

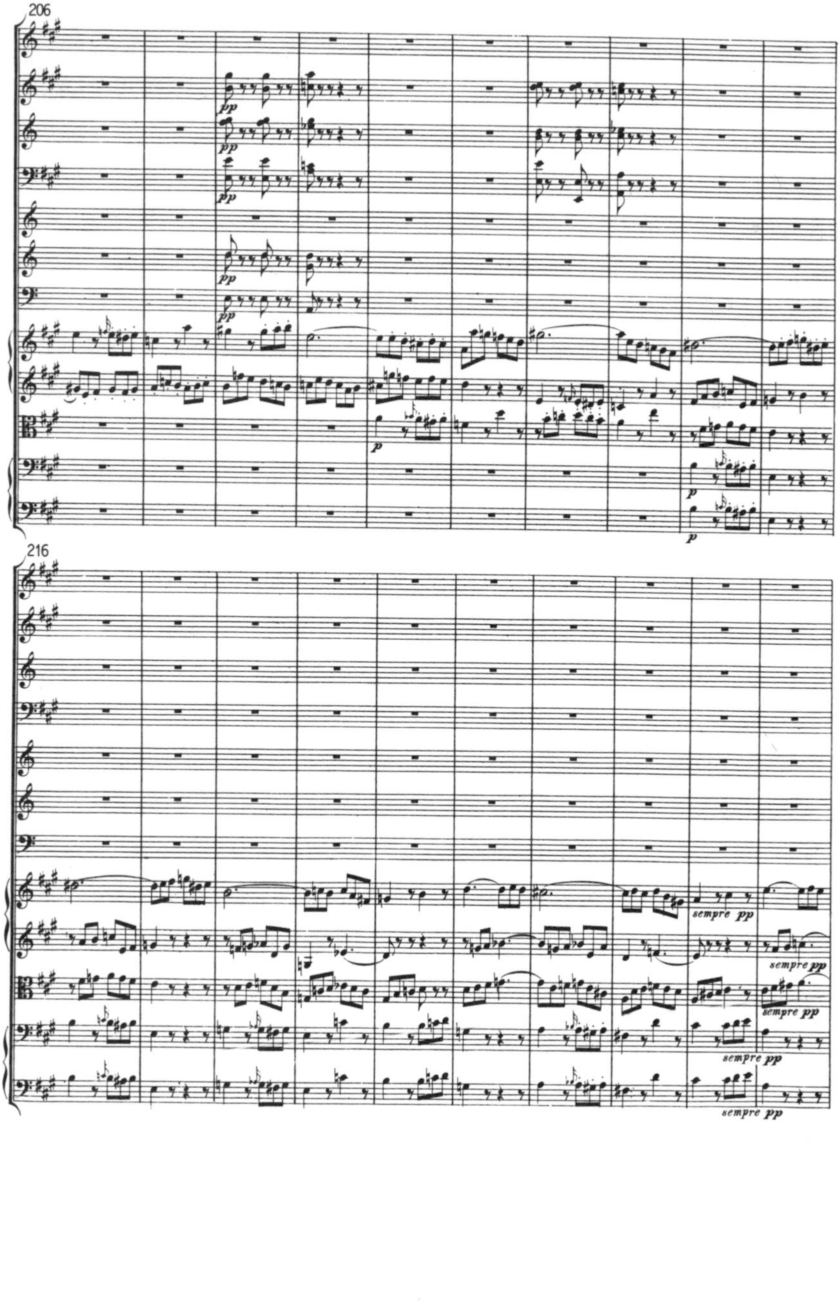
206
pp
p
216
sempre pp

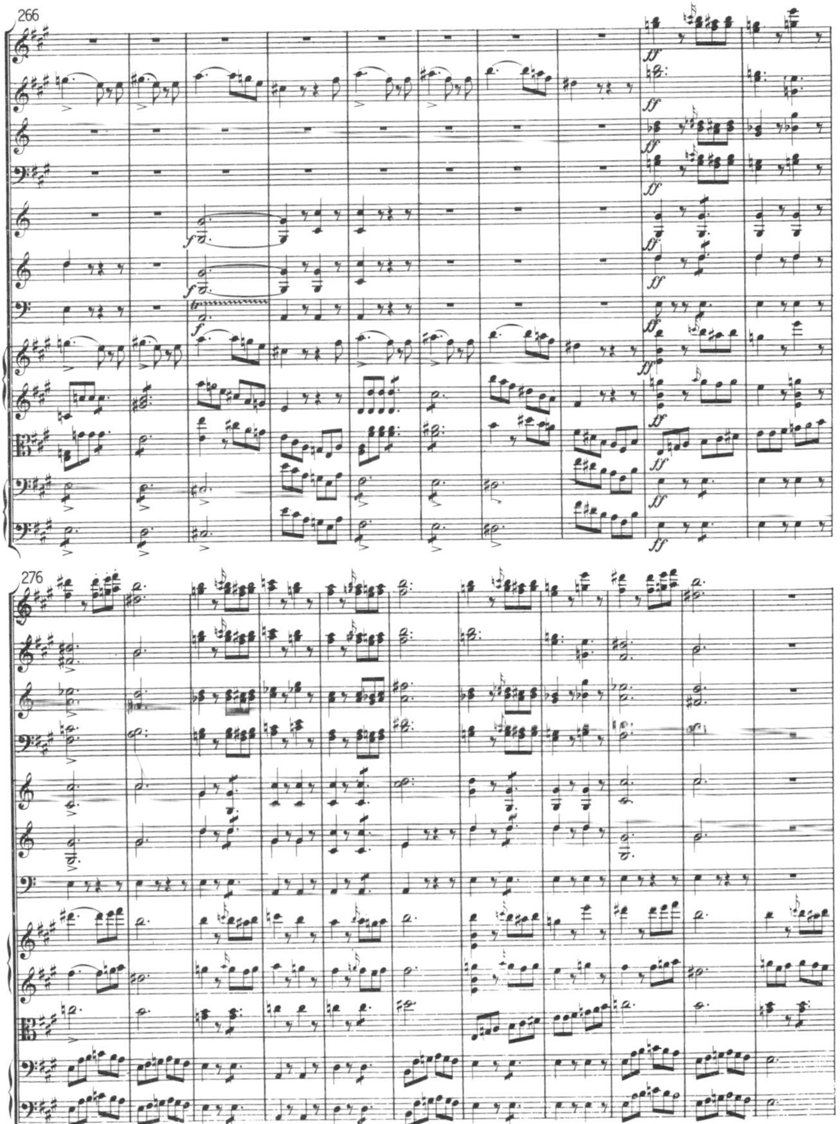
266
276

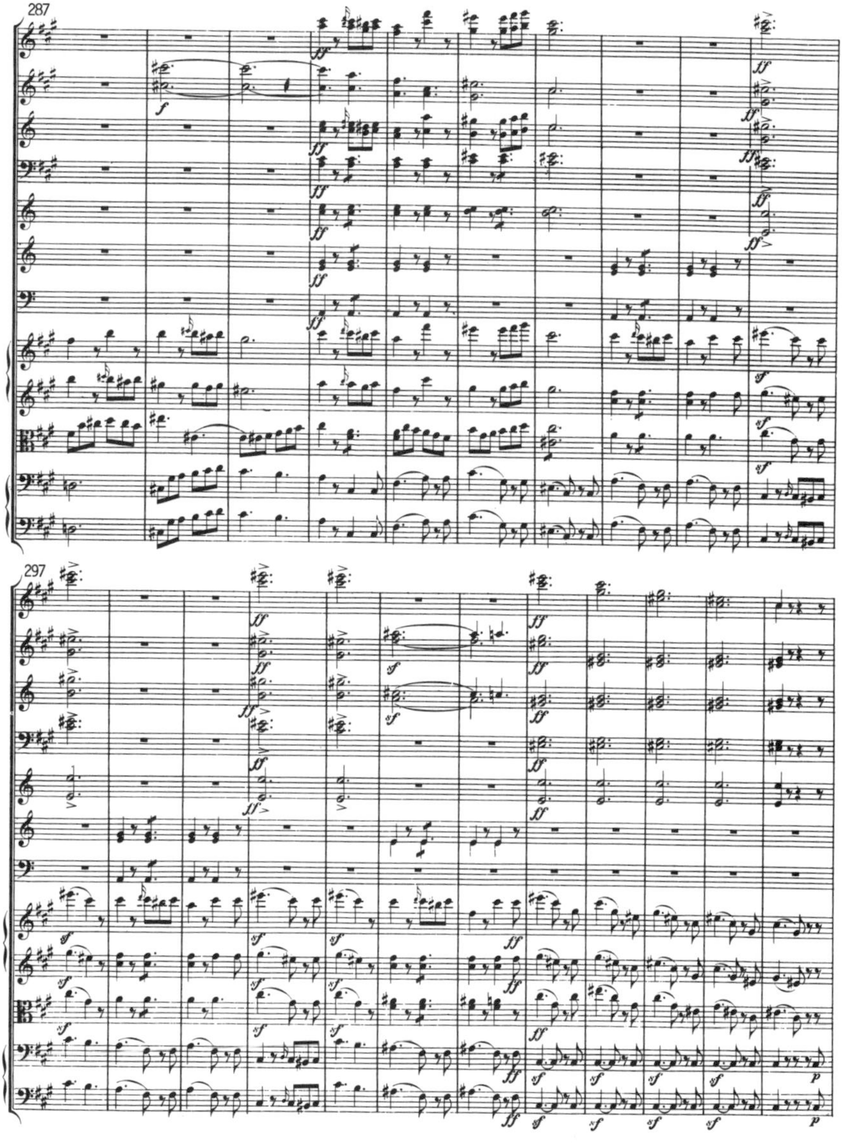
287
297

334
cresc.
mf
cresc.
sf
f
sf
poco a poco cresc.
mf
cresc.
p cresc.
cresc.
poco a poco cresc.
cresc.
poco a poco cresc.
mf
cresc.
f
poco a poco cresc.
344
D
f
sf
p
D

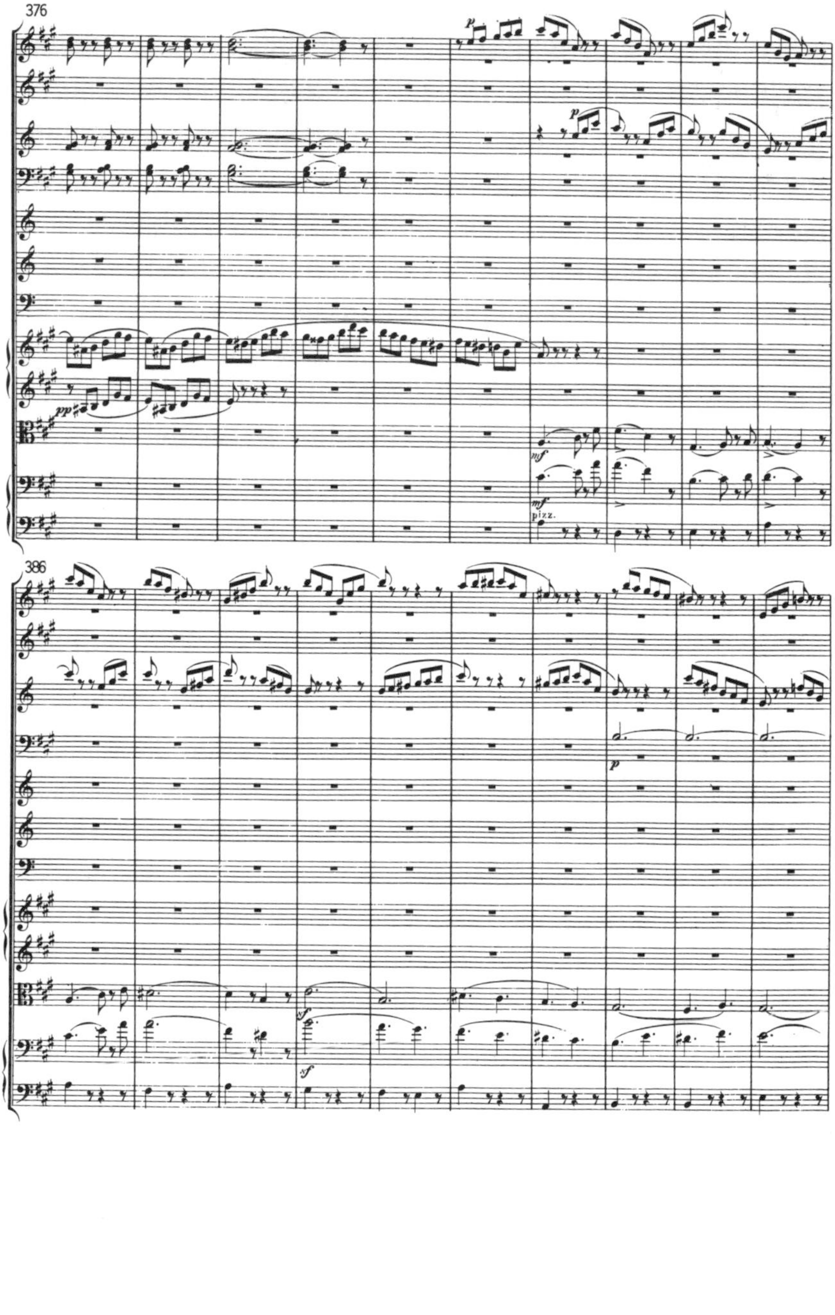
376
p
p
pp
mf
mf
pizz.
386
p
sf
sf

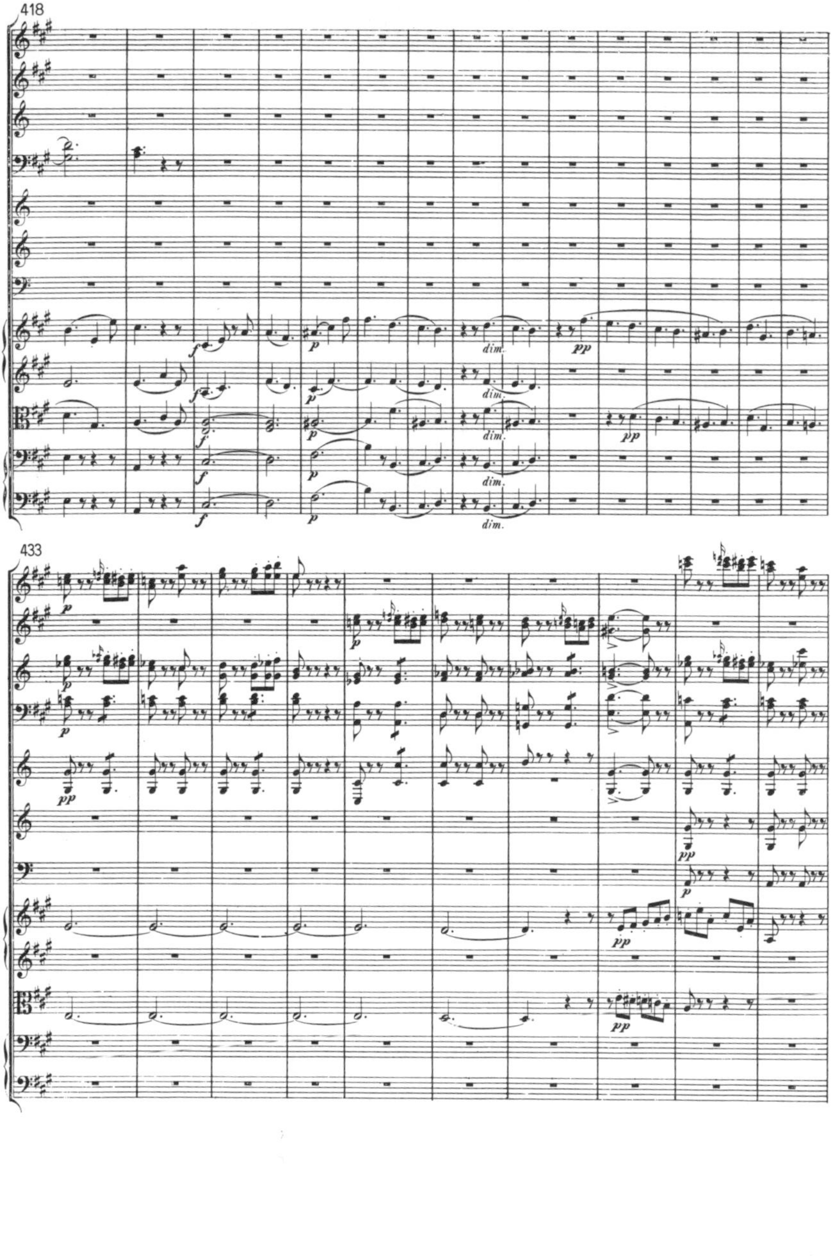
418
f
p
dim.
pp
433
pp

29

35

43

46

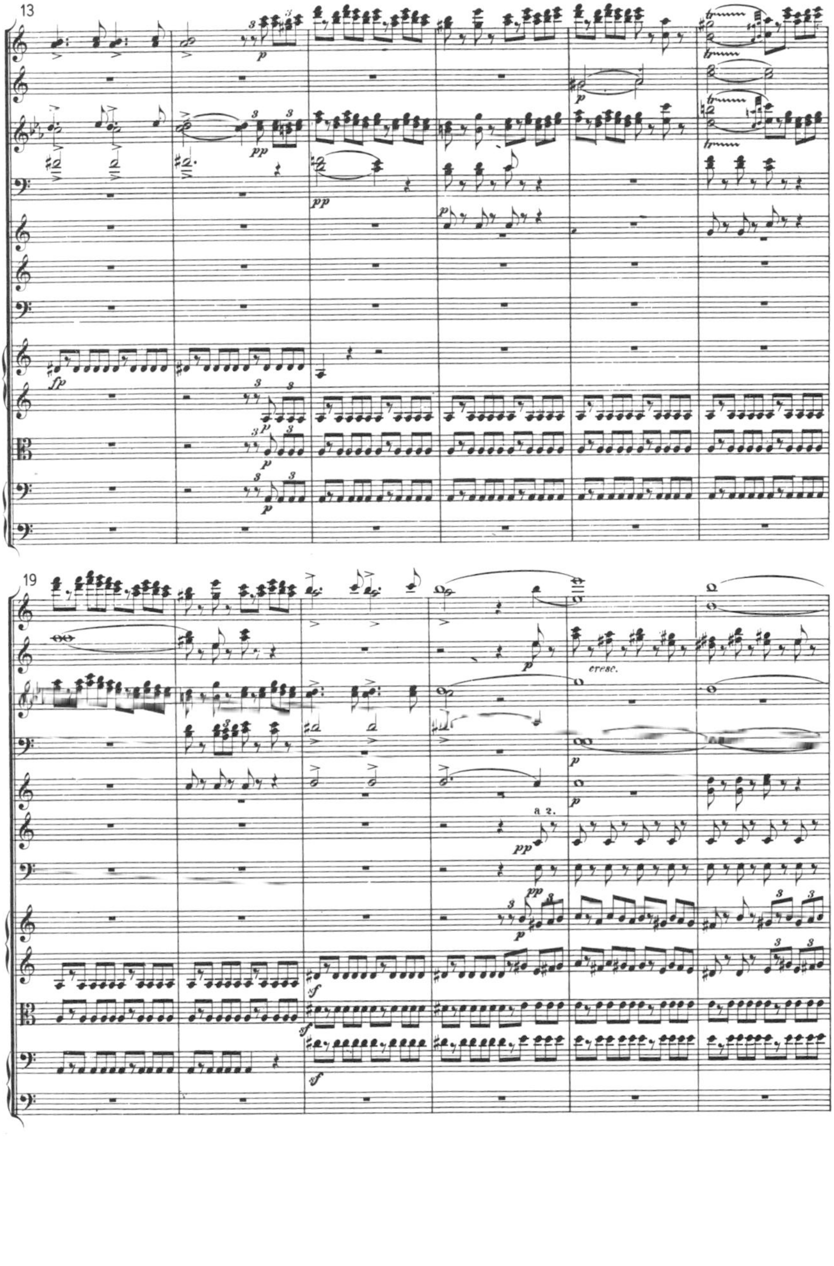
13
19
cresc.
a 2.

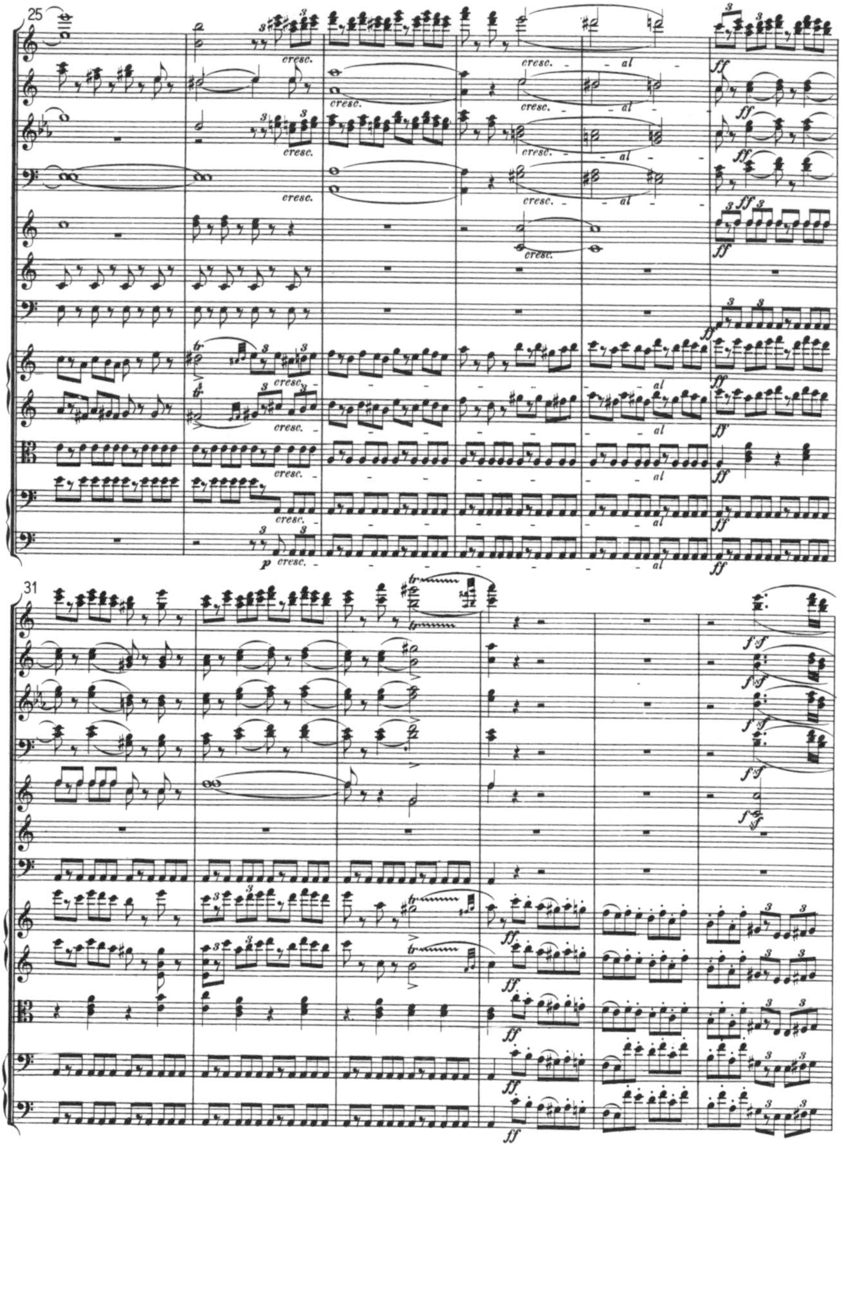
25
cresc.
al
ff
tr
p
31
f

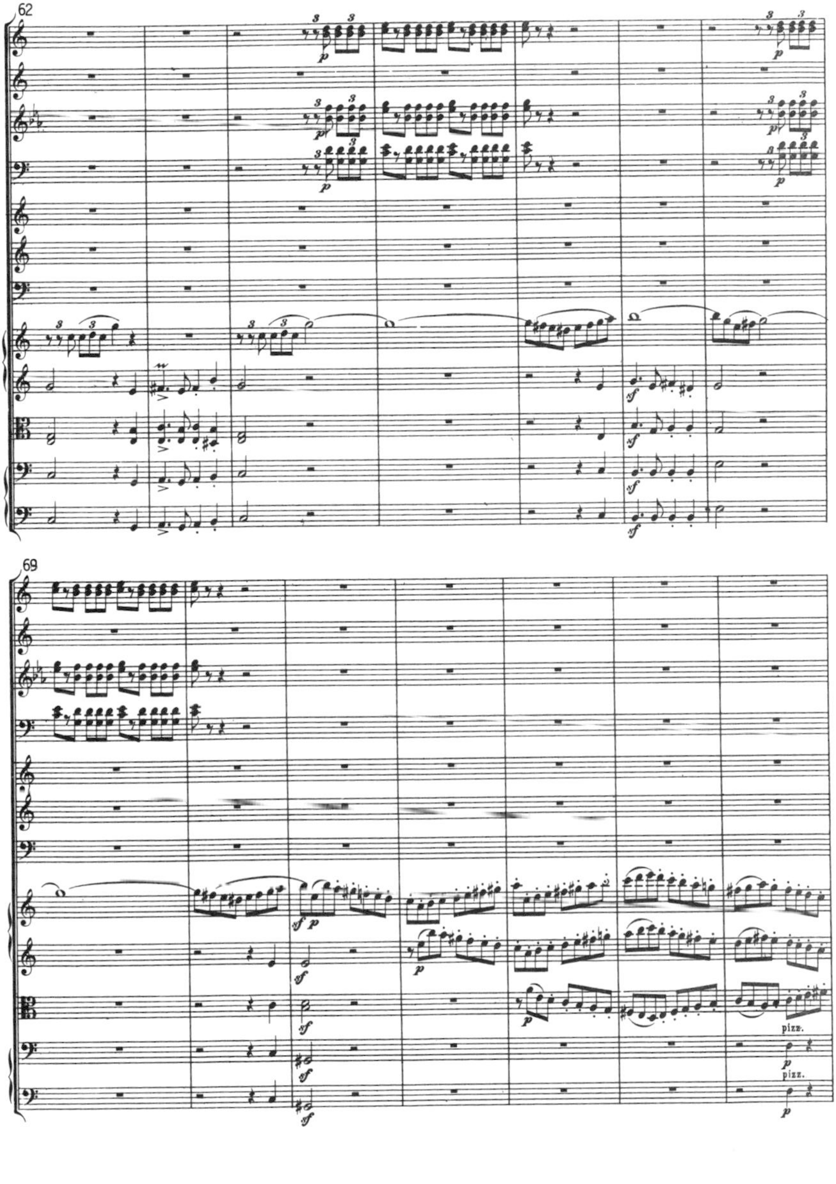
62
69
pizz.
pizz.

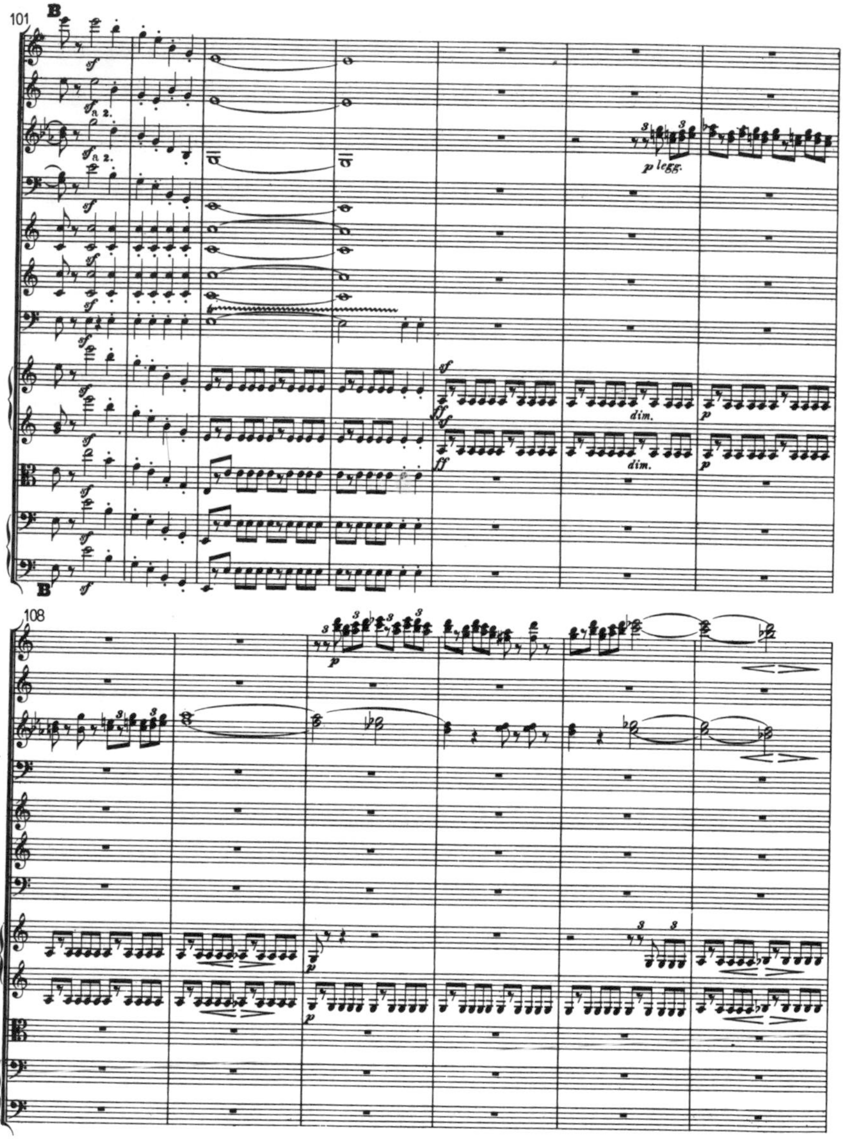
101
B
sf
a 2.
p legg.
ff
dim.
p
108

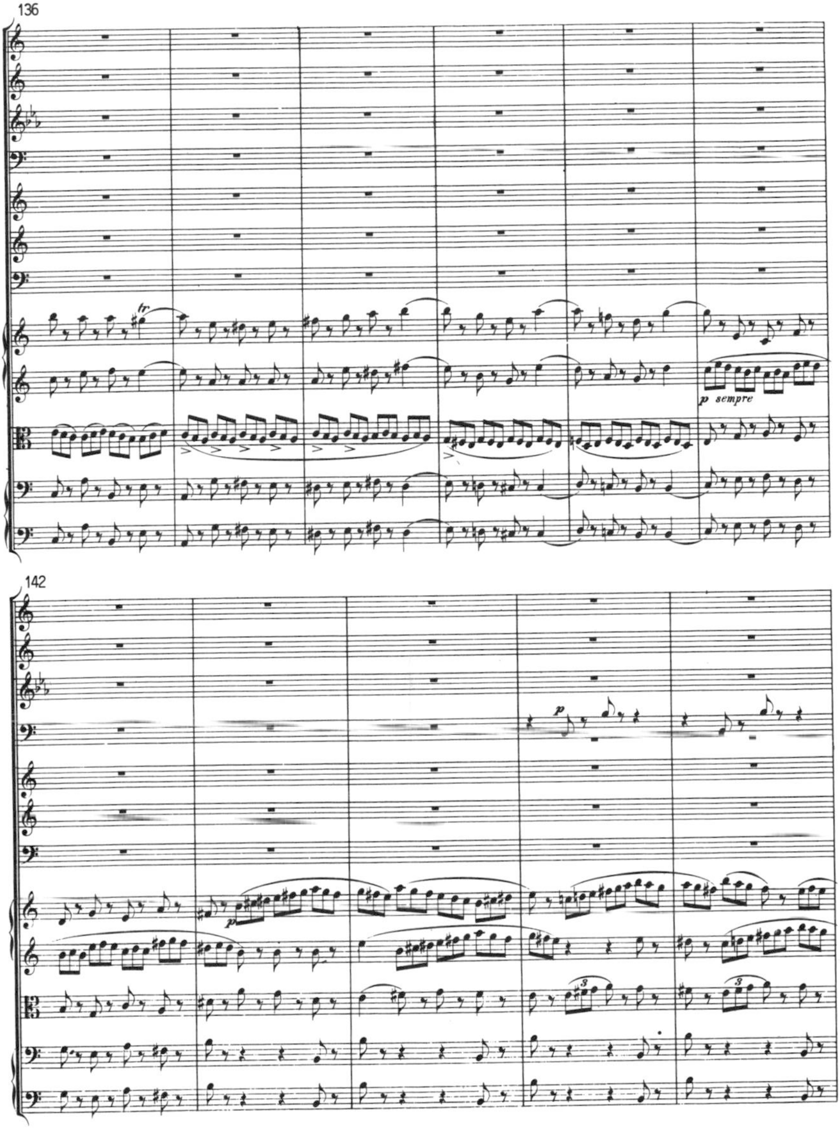
136
tr
p sempre
142
p
3

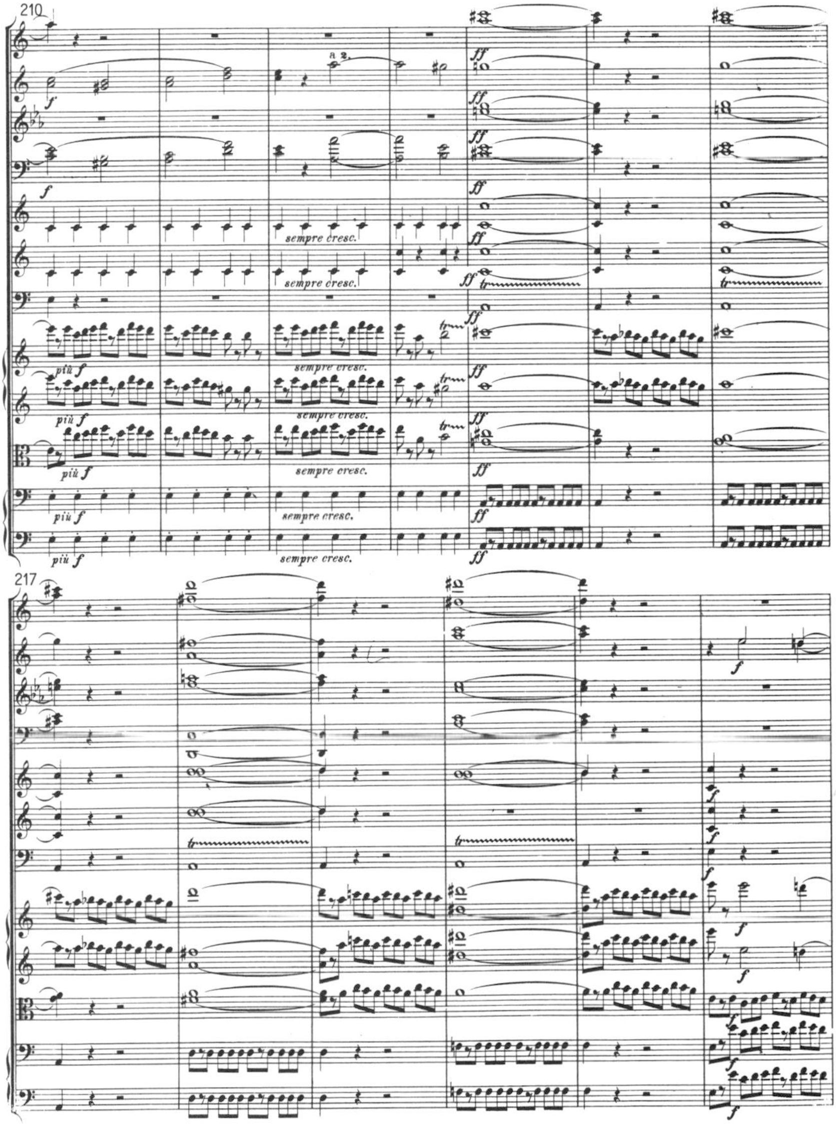
210
a 2.
sempre cresc.
più f
217

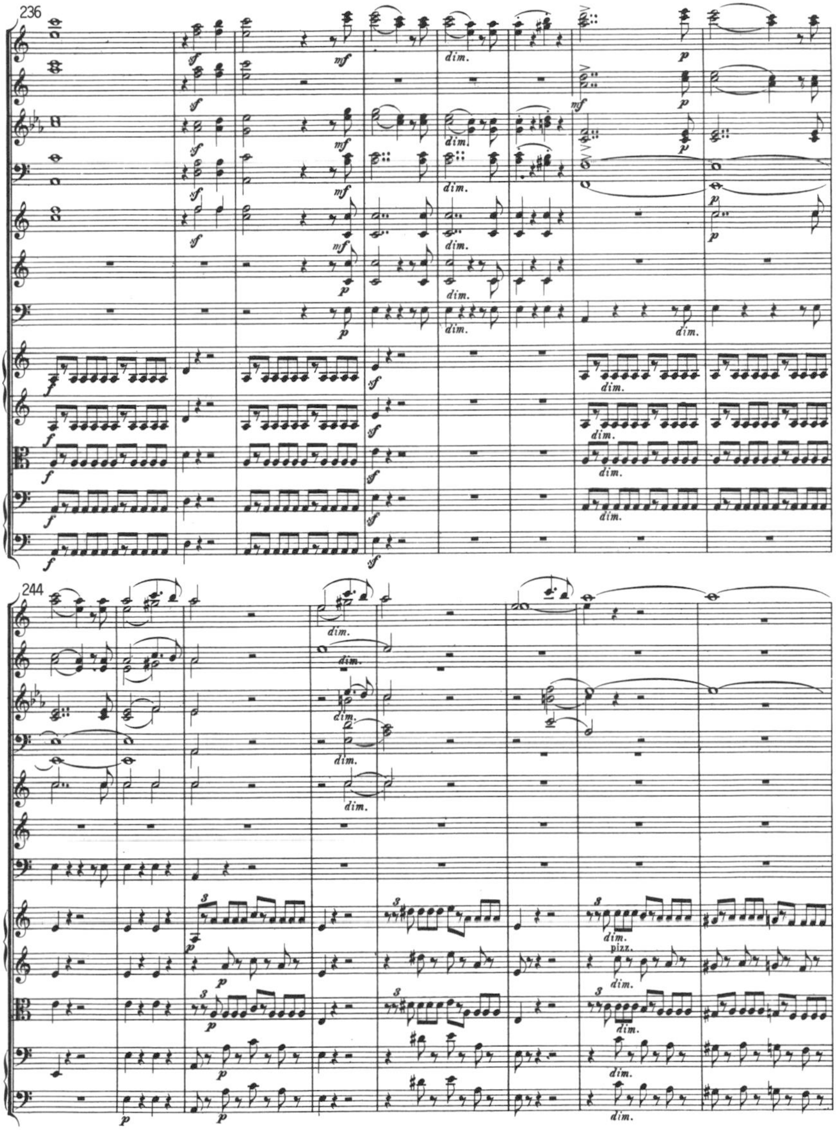
236
244
dim.
pizz.
mf
p
f

END OF EDITION

DOVER FULL-SIZE ORCHESTRAL SCORES

THE SIX BRANDENBURG CONCERTOS AND THE FOUR ORCHESTRAL SUITES IN FULL SCORE, Johann Sebastian Bach. Complete standard Bach-Gesellschaft editions in large, clear format. Study score. 273pp. 9 × 12. 23376-6 Pa. **$11.95**

COMPLETE CONCERTI FOR SOLO KEYBOARD AND ORCHESTRA IN FULL SCORE, Johann Sebastian Bach. Bach's seven complete concerti for solo keyboard and orchestra in full score from the authoritative Bach-Gesellschaft edition. 206pp. 9 × 12. 24929-8 Pa. **$11.95**

THE THREE VIOLIN CONCERTI IN FULL SCORE, Johann Sebastian Bach. Concerto in A Minor, BWV 1041; Concerto in E Major, BWV 1042; and Concerto for Two Violins in D Minor, BWV 1043. Bach-Gesellschaft edition. 64pp. 9⅜ × 12¼. 25124-1 Pa. **$6.95**

GREAT ORGAN CONCERTI, OPP. 4 & 7, IN FULL SCORE, George Frideric Handel. 12 organ concerti composed by great Baroque master are reproduced in full score from the *Deutsche Handelgesellschaft* edition. 138pp. 9⅜ × 12¼. 24462-8 Pa. **$8.95**

COMPLETE CONCERTI GROSSI IN FULL SCORE, George Frideric Handel. Monumental Opus 6 Concerti Grossi, Opus 3 and "Alexander's Feast" Concerti Grossi—19 in all—reproduced from most authoritative edition. 258pp. 9⅜ × 12¼. 24187-4 Pa. **$13.95**

LATER SYMPHONIES, Wolfgang A. Mozart. Full orchestral scores to last symphonies (Nos. 35-41) reproduced from definitive Breitkopf & Härtel Complete Works edition. Study score. 285pp. 9 × 12. 23052-X Pa. **$12.95**

PIANO CONCERTOS NOS. 17-22, Wolfgang Amadeus Mozart. Six complete piano concertos in full score, with Mozart's own cadenzas for Nos. 17-19. Breitkopf & Härtel edition. Study score. 370pp. 9⅜ × 12¼. 23599-8 Pa. **$16.95**

PIANO CONCERTOS NOS. 23-27, Wolfgang Amadeus Mozart. Mozart's last five piano concertos in full score, plus cadenzas for Nos. 23 and 27, and the Concert Rondo in D Major, K.382. Breitkopf & Härtel edition. Study score. 310pp. 9⅜ × 12¼. 23600-5 Pa. **$13.95**

DAPHNIS AND CHLOE IN FULL SCORE, Maurice Ravel. Definitive full-score edition of Ravel's rich musical setting of a Greek fable by Longus is reprinted here from the original French edition. 320pp. 9⅜ × 12¼. (Not available in France or Germany) 25826-2 l Pa. **$15.95**

THREE GREAT ORCHESTRAL WORKS IN FULL SCORE, Claude Debussy. Three favorites by influential modernist: *Prélude à l'Après-midi d'un Faune, Nocturnes,* and *La Mer.* Reprinted from early French editions. 279pp. 9 × 12. 24441-5 Pa. **$13.95**

SYMPHONY IN D MINOR IN FULL SCORE, César Franck. Superb, authoritative edition of Franck's only symphony, an often-performed and recorded masterwork of late French romantic style. 160pp. 9 × 12. 25373-2 Pa. **$9.95**

THE GREAT WALTZES IN FULL SCORE, Johann Strauss, Jr. Complete scores of eight melodic masterpieces: The Beautiful Blue Danube, Emperor Waltz, Tales of the Vienna Woods, Wiener Blut, four more. Authoritative editions. 336pp. 8⅜ × 11¼. 26009-7 Pa. **$14.95**

THE FIREBIRD IN FULL SCORE (Original 1910 Version), Igor Stravinsky. Handsome, inexpensive edition of modern masterpiece, renowned for brilliant orchestration, glowing color. Authoritative Russian edition. 176pp. 9⅜ × 12¼. (Available in U.S. only) 25535-2 Pa. **$10.95**

PETRUSHKA IN FULL SCORE: Original Version, Igor Stravinsky. The definitive full-score edition of Stravinsky's masterful score for the great Ballets Russes 1911 production of *Petrushka.* 160pp. 9⅜ × 12¼. (Available in U.S. only) 25680-4 Pa. **$9.95**

MAJOR ORCHESTRAL WORKS IN FULL SCORE, Felix Mendelssohn. Generally considered to be Mendelssohn's finest orchestral works, here in one volume are: the complete *Midsummer Night's Dream; Hebrides Overture; Calm Sea and Prosperous Voyage Overture;* Symphony No. 3 in A ("Scottish"); and Symphony No. 4 in A ("Italian"). Breitkopf & Härtel edition. Study score. 406pp. 9 × 12. 23184-4 Pa. **$18.95**

Available from your music dealer or write for
free Music Catalog to Dover Publications, Inc., Dept. MUBI,
31 East 2nd Street, Mineola, N.Y. 11501.